HOW TO SNEAK MORE YOGA INTO YOUR LIFE

K. Kris Loomis

K. Kris Loomis

ISBN: 9781520121031
ASIN: B01FSVTY02

How to Sneak More Yoga Into Your Life

K. Kris Loomis

Dedication

For Hugh. You are the best and I thank you for your patience, love, and encouragement without which I could not have written this book.

K. Kris Loomis

Author's Note

I would like to thank my beta readers, Hugh Loomis (my most ardent supporter and fan), Angela Hardin (I can always count on her to buy my chairs), and Joyce Sanders (one of my favorite potters). This book would not have been possible without your valuable feedback!

Introduction

I never set out to study yoga. But when I did have the opportunity to explore yoga, I ran into the same problems that most people do after they've taken a few classes. I remember thinking, now what? I knew I needed to "practice," but had no idea how to begin. How do people improve if they don't have time to practice, or know HOW to practice in the first place? After many years of personal experience and teaching, I realized how easy it is to address this problem, so I wrote this book to share with you what has worked for me and many of my students.

My yoga journey began when a friend of mine invited me to go to a yoga class with her. She was a geriatric nurse and had read some studies about the benefits of introducing yoga therapy to older patients. She was interested in the possibility of boosting the quality of her patients' lives by helping them improve their stability and lung function.

To be honest, I wasn't really interested in yoga at that time, thinking it was a lot of new-age mumbo-jumbo. I envisioned a lot of hippies chanting while sitting in painful pretzel positions in a room stinking of incense. I did not think that scenario was for me, but I thought, at the worst, we would have a fun topic of conversation over a bottle of wine sometime. So I accepted her invitation.

The class was held at a local arts center by a quiet woman who was just beginning her teacher training. She did burn incense (not so "stinky" after all) but there would be no chanting that day. Among the vivid paintings of local Southern artists, the afternoon came to life with yoga dogs and frogs and trees and geometrical shapes that felt exhilarating and liberating to my tight muscles. I became dizzy from my breath. At one point I broke a sweat. This was not what I was expecting. I walked into that class a skeptic and walked out a student of yoga for life.

I continued going to classes and began dabbling with yoga at home. I would try to recreate what we had done in class each week, but found, not only was it difficult to remember the postures and sequences, it was also difficult to find a decent block of time to practice. Inevitably, the phone would ring. My husband would walk through the room inquiring about dinner. My dog would plop down in the middle of my mat demanding a belly rub. And shouldn't I be putting that other load of clothes in the dryer?

After I started teaching, I heard similar complaints from my students. Seems that everyone these days is swamped with house stuff, kid stuff, garden stuff, relationship stuff, in-law stuff, with no time left for yoga stuff.

A couple of years passed, and I had not been able to give any better advice to my students than, "Just keep trying to set aside 15 minutes a day." And, honestly, with a full-time job and teaching several yoga classes a week, I barely had time for my own practice. It was becoming more and more difficult for me to follow my own advice.

Then one day I began to realize that my yoga practice had

started sneaking up on me away from the mat. I would find myself in Mountain pose while standing in line at the grocery store. I would automatically go into a seated twist if I had been at my desk too long. I instinctively altered my breath anytime I felt anxious or nervous. I found that five minutes were better than no minutes. And, in a pinch, even one minute would suffice.

Could it really be this easy to incorporate yoga into my hectic life? Could I count this as "practice?" Did yoga have to be a "separate" part of my life? The day I answered "no" to that last question was the day I started living my yoga. I now use every chance I get to sneak a little yoga in, no matter where or how busy I am. A little yoga is definitely better than no yoga!

I think that when we start studying yoga, we tend to focus on what we can't do rather than on what we can do. We see the pictures in magazines and websites of svelte yogis in impossibly difficult positions and forget that yoga is not about doing the difficult, but about doing something good for ourselves. I wrote this book so that you can see, with a few hacks and a willingness to try, how easy it is to integrate real yoga into your life. Not the kind that will wow the masses, but the kind that quantifiably contributes to your better physical and mental well-being.

How to Use This Book

I have divided this book into four sections, each section focusing on a different aspect of the practice. First, we will explore various ways to improve the quality of your breath with five simple breathing techniques. Then we will look at some physical postures, or asanas, beginning with a few standing postures. These will help you tone and strengthen your legs, and also allow you to work safely on your balance. If you have a desk job you will want to pay special attention to the section on seated postures. I conclude the book with some floor exercises that are a boon for back health.

You could work through the book by trying to add an exercise a day, getting through the book in less than a month, or you may prefer to work on incorporating a section a week. Or you might find yourself jumping around, and that's fine, too. Once you see how easy it is to make yoga a real part of your life, you will want to get through the book as quickly as possible.

Your first homework is to start identifying the "empty zones" in your life. These are times when you are stuck between tasks, waiting for something, or just plain bored. "Empty zones" are golden moments to a yogi. What if you consciously filled 30 one-minute "empty zones" in your day with yoga? That amounts to 30 minutes of practice without having to set aside any special time apart from the rest of your day. Who said the 30 minutes had to be consecutive?

Recent studies have shown that our exercise can be divided into smaller chunks throughout the day, so do what you can, when you can. A little yoga goes a long way, so just sneak it in and don't feel guilty about not getting a whole 30 minutes in at one stretch. It all adds up, so no excuses!

I will also address the concept of using "triggers" to help you remember to do certain postures. A trigger is anything that you can use to remind you to do something. I will focus on external triggers, like the phone ringing, a car honk, a crying baby, or even a particular word. Along with assessing your "empty zones," you will want to begin thinking of possible triggers that you can apply to your own practice. Keep this simple. Just think of things that happen on a fairly regular basis in your life that you could use as a signal to do a breathing exercise or spend a few breaths in a yoga posture.

I have tried to keep the language of the book simple, and although you will find some Sanskrit names for postures along the way, I have made sure to include the common English equivalents. Having the Sanskrit term will make it easier for you to look up postures if you need additional references.

Above all, you will want to keep a flexible mind. Some of the suggestions will be fairly easy to integrate, others may be more challenging. Take what works for you and don't worry about the rest because you may be able to incorporate them at a later time. Some days will be better than others, but before you know it, yoga will have snuck into your daily life just like it snuck into mine!

CHAPTER ONE
Breathing Exercises

Introduction to the Breathing Exercises

I chose to begin this book with the chapter on breathing because incorporating conscious breath on a daily basis opens the door for other aspects of yoga to sneak in. Inhaling is the only way our bodies can obtain oxygen, and exhaling is one of the body's main ways of expelling toxins, so breathing is one of the most important things to practice when it comes to yoga, or for that matter, life.

Yoga breathing is almost always done through the nose. Our noses are great filtration systems, so breathing through the nose is a great way to prevent larger particles from entering the lungs. I have an older male student that says, "I've got one hell of a filter!" Of course, in life, there are always exceptions. But unless I mention otherwise, assume you should breathe in and out through the nose.

Breathing through the nose also has a calming effect, which helps with focus when faced with a difficult situation or while attempting a challenging posture. Some special breathing techniques, such as the "Ujjayi" breath, also known as the "ocean" or "victorious" breath, create a resistance for you to breathe against, helping you to build pulmonary strength, which can help with endurance.

The breathing exercises in this book are simple and can be practiced by anyone. Some are more energizing, so you may want to focus on them in the mornings. Others are better suited for the evening because they can be very relaxing. Once you find an exercise that works for you, USE IT. Use it every chance you get, even if it's while you are waiting for your food to warm up in the microwave!

Breathing Awareness

WHY SHOULD YOU PRACTICE BREATHING AWARENESS?

Because this breathing exercise will give you a great mental break! It is also the absolute easiest exercise in the book and can be practiced anywhere, by anyone, with no fuss.

HOW TO DO IT:

This exercise uses your "normal" breathing, your day to day reflex breath. While practicing this exercise you do not want to manipulate or control your breath in any way. It can be performed standing, sitting, or while lying down. You will be successful whether you observe one breath or twenty.

This is about awareness, not manipulation. Do not try to change your breath. Let it be what it is in that moment. All you have to do is observe your breath as if you were a bystander watching someone else breathe.

Notice how the body physically changes to accommodate the breath. Can you feel the actual shape of your body change? Do you feel more movement in your belly, or in your chest? Any movement in the rib-cage? Can you feel the air as it enters the nostrils? Can you feel it brush against the back of your throat? What is the temperature of the air as it enters the body? As it exits the body? Your breath will probably change once you start paying attention to it. Notice that too.

HOW TO SNEAK IT IN:

This simple, yet powerful, exercise is like a mini-vacation for your mind, so use it anytime you are feeling mentally bogged down at work or school, or anytime you are feeling stressed. You can also practice this technique during various "empty zones" in your day, such as waiting for someone to answer the phone, waiting on a fax or text, waiting for your car to warm up on a cold morning, or waiting in line at the bank. We spend a huge portion of our day waiting. Might as well do something positive and productive with that time, right?

My trigger for the Breathing Awareness exercise is the phone. Anytime the phone rings, I notice one conscious breath before I answer it. I encourage you to keep thinking about the use of triggers in your own life and how you might use them as you work through this book.

Belly Breathing

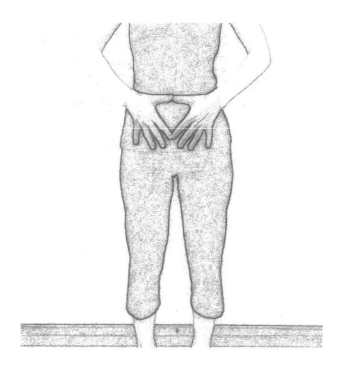

WHY SHOULD YOU PRACTICE BELLY BREATHING?

Because Belly Breathing, aka Abdominal Breathing, is a great way to exercise your diaphragm while producing a deep sense of calm and relaxation. This is a super method to use if you suffer from high blood pressure or anxiety. You can see the process in action if you have small children or pets. Watch their tummies while they sleep. Observe the easy rising and falling. Imagine how soft their tummies are! Then notice your own breath. Different, huh? But don't worry. With a little practice, you can be breathing like a child.

HOW TO DO IT:

The easiest way to learn to belly breathe is to touch your thumbs together, place them on your belly button, then let your hands rest over your abdomen. Spread your fingers apart! You want to cover as much of your abdomen as possible.

Now take a few slow, deep breaths. Imagine that you are breathing into your hands, as if your lungs were actually located under your palms. That's all there is to it! Once you get the hang of it, you will not need to place your hands on your abdomen because you will be feeling the movement from the inside out.

Belly Breathing can be done while standing or sitting, but my favorite way to practice Belly Breathing is while lying down.

HOW TO SNEAK IT IN:

Because of the calming nature of this exercise, it is perfect to slip into a hectic day. On the way to a meeting? Belly breathe in the elevator. Got a big exam? Belly breathe while the teacher is handing out the test. About to say something you might regret? Stop and take three deep belly breaths. If you have a baby or small child, why not use his or her crying as a trigger for belly breathing? As you try to soothe your child you will definitely feel calmer.

Matched Inhale/Exhale

WHY SHOULD YOU PRACTICE MATCHED INHALE/EXHALE BREATHING?

Because this type of breathing helps focus the mind, as well as provide a balanced structure for repetitive activities, exercise, or sports. This exercise takes us into the realm of controlled breathing where you will actively manipulate your breath.

HOW TO DO IT:

Simply match the length of your inhale and exhale. Inhale to a count of 4, exhale to a count of 4. Inhale to a count of 8, exhale to a count of 8. Easy!

HOW TO SNEAK IT IN:

This breathing is a great complement to active sports such as running, swimming, cycling, and Vinyasa Yoga. Try to match your pace to your breath, and vice-versa. For example, you could run four paces to the inhale and four paces to the exhale. Or in yoga, one movement per inhale, one movement per exhale, like in the sun salutations. Take arms above your head on an inhale, fold forward (bend forward at the hips) on an exhale. Over time, this makes your movements very fluid and controlled.

So what should you do if you aren't into running or more active sports? Use this breath when you hammer, when you knit, or when you are tenderizing your steak for dinner. Any repetitive motion will do.

But I have found that one of the easiest ways to fit this matched breathing exercise into your life is to do it while walking. Walking to the car, walking into school or work, walking around the mall. Inhale-step-step-step, exhale-step-step-step. If you can walk, you can practice this exercise. No excuses!

Ujjayi, or Ocean Breath

WHY SHOULD YOU PRACTICE THE OCEAN BREATH?

Because this is a great way to exercise your lungs. This type of breathing can be used in conjunction with the Matched Inhale/Exhale for an extra oomph!

HOW TO DO IT:

Even though Ujjayi is often referred to as the "ocean" or "victorious" breath, I like to call it the "Darth Vader" breath. You'll know what I mean if you ever hear a strong breather perform it!

Keep in mind that this breath is done through the nose, but while trying to get comfortable with the technique you will begin by exhaling through the mouth. Take a deep breath in through your nose, then as you exhale through your mouth make a soft "hhaaa" sound as if you were trying to fog a mirror. Repeat, but this time gently close your lips halfway through the exhale. Notice that the exhale and sound transfer to the nose. Keep a little space between your top and bottom teeth and imagine you have a small egg at the back of your mouth near the entrance to your throat.

Once you have mastered the exhale, keep all the parts in place as you try to imitate the sound on the inhale. You will feel a little constriction at the back of your throat. When I practice Ujjayi breathing I feel like the breath enters and exits through the front of my throat, not my nose. You will know you've got the hang of it if you can hear the ocean. Or Darth Vader.

HOW TO SNEAK IT IN:

This is the type of breath specifically called for in more athletic styles of yoga, such as Ashtanga or Vinyasa. But you can sneak it into your regular life anytime you are feeling a little stressed. Like in a traffic jam. Or when your kid gets in trouble at school. Or after an argument with your significant other. You will find that the gentle sound of this style of breathing can be very soothing.

Progressive Relaxation

WHY SHOULD YOU PRACTICE PROGRESSIVE RELAXATION?

Because it is a beautiful way to end your day. Although Progressive Relaxation is more than a breathing exercise, I wanted to include it here because it teaches the value of working with your exhale. Plus, this exercise puts the body in a state this is more receptive to sleep, which is something most people will welcome. It can also be used as a beginning meditation exercise.

HOW TO DO IT:

You can do this on the floor, or right after you have gone to bed. Lie on your back, preferably with your legs straight. Your arms should be by your sides with the palms facing up.

You will work systematically through your body. As you inhale through the nose, you will tighten a part of the body, then as you exhale through the mouth with a soft "haa," you will release the tension. Repeat three times for each body part.

Begin with your feet. As you inhale, spread your toes as far apart as you can, then on the exhale relax your toes and feet. Repeat two more times. Then move your awareness to your thighs. Inhale, tighten your thighs, exhale, release the tension. Then your butt. Inhale, clench, exhale, relax. Remember to repeat each of these for a total of three breath cycles. Next, focus on your hands. As you inhale open your palms and spread your fingers as far apart as possible, then relax them as you exhale. Move up your arms.

Inhale, contract your biceps and triceps, exhale and allow those muscles to soften. Finally take your attention to your face. As you inhale, open your mouth wide like you are initiating a yawn, but as you exhale, relax you face and imagine the skin of your face becoming very smooth and soft.

You can use a matched breathing pattern if you wish, or your normal breathing. Remember to inhale slowly through the nose as you contract, but exhale through the mouth with a soft "haa" as you release the tension.

HOW TO SNEAK IT IN:

As I mentioned earlier, this is a great way to relax before bedtime. Also, use this if you wake up in the middle of the night and have trouble getting back to sleep. It gives the mind something to focus on while gently reminding the body that it is time to recharge.

If you have a mind that tends to race, this is a great diversion technique. This exercise can be practiced anytime you are under extreme pressure and find your body tensing up or your jaw clenched. Just make sure you have enough time to thoroughly work through the exercise. You don't want to have to jump up suddenly to go pick your daughter up from soccer practice! If you do the exercise properly, you will feel a little groggy afterward, so take care.

CHAPTER TWO
Standing Postures

Introduction to the Standing Postures

Now that you have a better understanding of how to "sneak" some breathing exercises into your day, it's time to find a place for the physical postures, or asanas. The postures I've chosen for this book are achievable by practically everyone. If you are a more advanced practitioner, the postures presented in the book will give you a chance to return to the "beginner's mind" often and shore up the foundational aspects of the practice. Sometimes just keeping in touch with simple postures daily is enough to keep you motivated to make that next class. If you are new to the practice of yoga, this is a great way for you to build confidence and a solid foundation without being overwhelmed.

You can choose to practice the Matched Inhale/Exhale breathing exercise along with the physical postures, or you can use your normal breathing. Just remember to breathe!

Tadasana, or Mountain

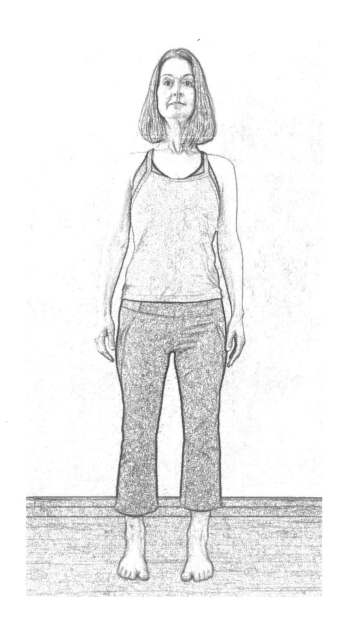

WHY SHOULD YOU PRACTICE MOUNTAIN?

Because this is one of the most important postures in the standing repertoire. It develops strength in the legs and ankles, it tackles posture problems, and it sets the foundation for all the other standing postures.

HOW TO DO IT:

Stand with your feet under your hips. Make sure that your feet are parallel to each other, meaning that the *outside* edges of your feet are parallel. Most people stand with their toes turned out, and often walk that way, too. This can cause pinching in the sacrum area and over time result in sciatic problems, so always look down and check if your feet are parallel. Some people feel a little strange when they stand like this at first, but you will get the hang of it, I promise!

Now gently rock forward and back a couple of times. You want to eventually come to stillness toward the back of your feet, about where the arch meets the heel. Your toes should not be gripping, but resting comfortably on the floor. Ideally, this posture should be done in bare feet, so do it that way when you are at home or in class. But I practice this posture EVERYWHERE, even when I am wearing shoes.

This posture uses what is commonly known as a static contraction. Basically, you want to contract your thigh muscles and keep them engaged. This helps stabilize and strengthen the muscles around the knees as well as the quads. This used to be called "locking," but you should really just think of all the muscles of your thighs pressing in toward the thighbones. This action will give you the sense of "lifting" your kneecaps.

I would like to take the time here to remind you that you are three-dimensional. We tend to live our lives through the fronts of our bodies. We don't stop and consider our backs and sides unless we have an ache or pain there. Your thighs are three dimensional, so squeeze from every direction (front, back, inner, and outer) toward the bone when you practice Mountain. This is important. Remember that you are setting the stage for all other standing postures by developing concrete skills. Plus, this is a fantastic injury preventative when you graduate to more difficult standing and seated postures.

Along with the thigh engagement, you will want to stabilize your pelvis. This is easy to accomplish. While you feel your thighbones gently pressing back, imagine tucking your tailbone under like a naughty puppy that's just been caught scratching your new furniture. These two opposing forces will stabilize your pelvis. Just be careful not to clench your butt! You can definitely overdo this action so play with it until you find a nice balance that does not cause you to clench your butt, your teeth, or halt your breath.

To get your chest in the correct position put your thumbs in your armpits like you're struttin' your stuff. You will feel the sternum rise and your chest broaden. Now keep the chest lifted and lower your arms to your sides. Relax your arms and allow your hands to feel heavy.

Now all that's left is to imagine that you are trying to lift the crown of your head closer to the ceiling or sky, almost as if you have a string coming out of the top of your head and someone is tugging up on that string. Your neck should feel very long as you do this.

Keep the muscles of your face relaxed as you hold this position through several breathing cycles.

HOW TO SNEAK IT IN:

This posture can be done anywhere you stand. In line at the grocery store, the bank, the cafeteria, while pumping gas, you name it. And if you are holding something in your arms, take the opportunity to work on the bottom half of the posture. Just remember not to clench your butt!

If you are a business person, a good trigger for this pose is when you are introduced to someone new. Just as you hear the words, "I'd like to introduce…" go into a proud Mountain. Your good posture will surely impress.

Utkatasana, or Chair

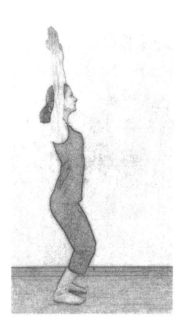

WHY SHOULD YOU PRACTICE THE CHAIR?

Because it is great for strengthening the thighs while stretching the lower calf and Achilles area. Chair is also classified as a gentle backbend, so you can receive the benefits of stimulating the nervous system while stretching the front of the torso and opening the chest while strengthening your back muscles and legs in this exercise.

As with most postures in yoga, there are many variations and modifications. My goal is to present the most accessible ones in relation to your regular life. When you are in a class situation, I hope you will explore the many variations of these postures.

HOW TO DO IT:

Start with your feet in the Mountain position. Slowly begin bending your knees and imagine that your back is sliding down a wall. Because you want to keep your heels on the floor you may not go down very far. That is not important. It is more important to try and keep your spine perpendicular to the floor, so don't hinge at the hips too much. And you would prefer that your knees don't knock together. Try to keep them in line with your ankles and hips. Keep your weight toward the back of the feet, just like in Mountain.

You might feel some tautness along your shins. You might also feel your mid and lower back muscles working. If so, good!

You can place your hands on your hips, raise them over your head, or let them hang by your sides. Your choice. Just try to keep that broad chest feel that you created in the Mountain posture earlier.

HOW TO SNEAK IT IN:

Chair is a great pose to practice in the kitchen. Waiting for something to heat up in the microwave? Practice chair. Waiting for water to boil? Practice chair. Filling a water bottle from the fridge? Practice chair. This one is super easy to sneak in!

Uttanasana, or Forward Fold

WHY SHOULD YOU PRACTICE THE FORWARD FOLD?

Because this is a great stretch for the back of your legs, especially if you sit a lot during the day. This will elongate your hamstrings and calves, strengthen your quads, and help you address the problem of weak back muscles.

HOW TO DO IT:

Begin in Mountain (remember that your feet should be parallel). Place your hands on your hips by putting your index and third fingers on your hipbones and wrapping your thumbs around back. Your hands should *not* be on your waist. Draw your shoulder blades closer to each other and feel your chest broaden.

You want to consciously keep in mind is that the front of your spine should stay as long as the back of your spine throughout the exercise. That means that you will not bend at the waist.

As you inhale, imagine the top of your head moving an inch closer to the ceiling, then as you exhale start hinging forward at the hip crease. Try to keep your weight toward the back of your feet, just like in Mountain.

Don't worry if you don't go too far. You want to go as far as you can, but not so far that you start holding your breath or clenching your teeth. Keep breathing!

If you feel tremendous pressure on the backs of your knees, you can micro-bend your knees, but you should keep your thighs engaged. Imagine that you are pushing your inner thighs toward the back of the room which will give you a little more space in the sacrum area of your lower back. You want to feel as if your tailbone is moving one direction and the crown of your head is moving in the opposite direction. You will feel the muscles of your mid back engage, especially if you manage to keep the front of your spine long.

Take several breaths, either the Matched Inhale/Exhale or your normal breathing, and work up to five or ten breaths. I like to imagine that my lungs are behind my hamstrings when I practice this posture. I know it sounds weird, but consciously breathing into the backs of your legs can really help encourage the muscles to eventually release allowing you to deepen the pose.

When you are ready to come out of this posture, do so with an inhale and keep that spine straight!

HOW TO SNEAK IT IN:

This posture is easy to sneak in when you are getting dressed. I try to practice it before I put my pants on in the morning then again after I get into my jammies at night. If you do it at those two times during the day you will notice that you are more flexible at night. Just an interesting way to be reminded of how our bodies don't just change from day to day, but also from hour to hour! Don't try to force your morning body to be like your evening body. If you consistently sneak this posture into your life twice a day you will soon see that your morning body will slowly start resembling your evening body.

Try not to worry too much about the outcome of these postures. Yoga is called a PRACTICE for a reason. Just fit these postures in as often as you can and don't worry about the results. You will gradually begin to notice that your instrument (your body) is becoming more in tune. A little yoga goes a long way!

Ardha Chandrasana, or Half Moon

WHY SHOULD YOU PRACTICE THE HALF MOON?

Because this is a wonderful exercise for the sides of the torso, hips, and legs. It is a perfect example of how opposition works in every posture, because as you contract and shorten one side of your body, you will feel the other side lengthening and stretching. As is the case with the other standing postures this pose also works on strengthening your legs.

The versions I present here are modifications of the full posture, which is one of the more advanced balance postures in the repertoire. Although I do practice the full version, this is the one that I sneak into my normal life.

HOW TO DO IT:

Start in Mountain (see how important Mountain is?) but instead of letting your arms rest by your side, activate them by pressing your palms into the outer thigh area and reaching your fingertips toward the floor.

While keeping the thighs engaged, slowly allow your right fingertips to slide closer to the floor as you begin to nudge your hips to the left. Do not take your hands off the sides of your body, but allow them to slide up and down alongside the thighs and hips. Go as far as you can, which doesn't have to be that far if you start feeling a good stretch on the left side of your body. After several breaths (again either the Matched Inhale/Exhale or normal breathing) come back upright and repeat on the other side.

To get more of a side stretch you can bring your feet together. Press the inner thighs towards each other. Reach up toward the ceiling with the left arm, palm in the direction of your head. You would love for your upper arm to be beside your ear, although not everyone is able to achieve that at first. As your right hand begins to slide down your outer right thigh and you find yourself in that nice half moon shape, reach actively with your left hand to the place across the room where the wall and ceiling meet. This will optimize your extension on that side while keeping the spine long. For an extra oomph, you can gently nudge your hips to the left.

HOW TO SNEAK IT IN:

This is one I like doing while I am waiting for my bath to fill up or for the water in my shower to get hot. But you can sneak it in almost anywhere else you would the other standing postures.

Vrksasana, or Tree

WHY SHOULD YOU PRACTICE THE TREE?

Because this is one of the best ways to start improving your balance. There are many reasons why people struggle with balance, ranging from sinus problems to weak muscle control to inadequate coordination between the two sides of the body. This posture helps you develop the tools to combat balance issues.

One of the most important things to do when you are practicing a balance posture is to set a *drishti*. This is simply a fixed focal point that you will look at while you are practicing the posture. You do not want your gaze to wander away from the spot you have chosen. It can be a spot on the wall or on the floor several feet in front of you. Some people find that the closer they are to their focal point the more stable they feel, so feel free to experiment with how far away you are from your *drishti* as you work on your balance.

Also be aware that it is common to have really good balance one day and struggle with it the next. So if it doesn't go well one day, don't despair, but if it goes really well another day, don't get too cocky about it!

HOW TO DO IT:

Start in Tadasana, the Mountain. Make sure your feet are parallel. Gently sway side to side feeling your weight shift from one foot to the other. Keep your thighs engaged! Notice that when your weight is on your left leg, the right leg is not really bearing any of the weight load; instead, it acts more like a training wheel on a kid's bike. Once you have this feeling, you are halfway there!

You have many options as far as your arms and hands go, but I suggest you first practice with the palms together in front of your chest. It is important that you actively press all four corners of your palms together. When you do this action, you will feel your chest muscles engage. You will also feel energized in your upper back, shoulders, and arms. Might as well get the most out of the posture, right? Besides, pressing the hands together helps to stabilize you.

Now shift your weight onto your left foot, keeping the left leg straight. While staring intently at your *drishti*, prop your right heel on the inner left ankle, but keep your right toes on the floor. If you are feeling stable, you can place the right foot as high up the inner left leg as you comfortably can, although you will get all of the balance benefits even if you don't lift the right foot completely off the floor. Don't forget to breathe! After about five breaths, come back into Mountain and take two breaths. Then consciously shift your weight onto the right foot and repeat the process on the other side.

If you are having a really off balance day, you can do this posture near a chair or wall. Just place one of your fingers on the back of the chair or against the wall while maintaining your focal point, and that should help. You can place your other hand on your hip.

HOW TO SNEAK IT IN:

This is a good one to do right before you put on your shoes and right after you take them off. Unlike the Mountain, that can occasionally be practiced with shoes on, the Tree should always be practiced barefooted. You want your standing foot to feel the connection with the floor and imagine that it is really wide across the base of the toes. The wider the foundation the better, so try to spread your toes apart, too. Your feet will thank you, especially after being cramped in narrow shoes all day long!

CHAPTER THREE
Seated Postures

Introduction to the Seated Postures

We spend a great deal of time each day sitting. Whether we are at our desks, in the car, at the dinner table, or watching TV, we sit too much! We hear more and more practically every week about how this is not good for us, but let's face it, there are just some things you have to sit down for. So why not make the most out of it?

Seated Mountain

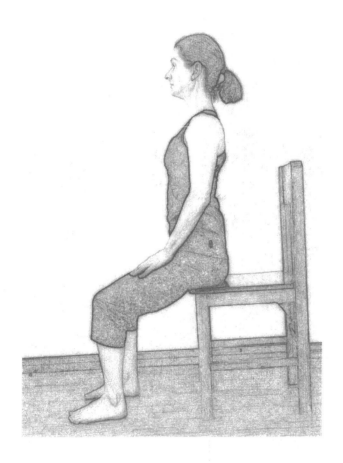

WHY SHOULD YOU PRACTICE THE SEATED MOUNTAIN?

Because this is an easy way to fine-tune your posture. Most people slump when they are seated, and this cramps the internal organs, especially the lungs. When the lungs don't have adequate space to expand, the whole body suffers from a lack of oxygen. This can cause a whole host of problems, not the least of which is tiredness. So sitting with good posture can help increase alertness, especially as the day wears on.

HOW TO DO IT:

Sit towards the front edge of your chair. You would like to feel your sit bones making firm contact with the seat of the chair. Do not lean back! Place your feet hip distance apart (flat on the floor) and make them parallel, just as if you were standing in Mountain. Feel your weight sink down through your sit bones while you lift the crown of your head up toward the ceiling. Remember the string in the standing version? Lift and broaden your sternum.

Relax your jaw, and take several deep breaths into your ribcage. Remember that you are three-dimensional, so try to expand the front, side, AND back ribs as you breathe. That's it!

HOW TO SNEAK IT IN:

This one is a life saver if you have a desk job. You may want to set an alarm on your phone or computer every 30 minutes to remind you to sneak it in. Or use an external trigger, like every time you get an email notification or before you check your social media. And because it does help increase your oxygen intake, it is a good one for students to do before a test or exam. A few good breaths are better than no good breaths!

Seated Cat/Cow

WHY SHOULD YOU PRACTICE THE SEATED CAT/COW?

Because this posture easily brings mobility to the spine, which is an important aspect of overall health. It also feels great to a stiff neck and tight hips.

HOW TO DO IT:

Begin in Seated Mountain. Place your hands' palms down on your knees. As you inhale, strongly lift your sternum and look up. Imagine that you are trying to lift your chin, nose, and forehead up to the ceiling. You do not want the head to drop all the way back. Draw your shoulder blades closer together. Then, on an exhale, round the back and tuck the chin towards the chest. During the forward bend portion of the exercise imagine that you are trying to pop your spine out toward the back of the chair. Repeat the process three to five times breathing slowly and coordinating the movement with the breath: inhale, look up, exhale, round the back and tuck the chin.

HOW TO SNEAK IT IN:

Being an extension of the Seated Mountain, why not tack it on right after you do that one? It will only add another 30 seconds, and trust me, it will be 30 seconds well spent. Not only are these seated postures beneficial if you have a desk job, they are great to practice if your plane is delayed and you are stuck at the airport.

Seated Twist

WHY SHOULD YOU PRACTICE THE SEATED TWIST?

Because our insides need as much attention as our outsides! Twists invigorate our internal organs, which can aid in digestion and elimination. Along with the Seated Cat/Cow, this posture also contributes to better spine and back mobility. And to top it off, twists stimulate circulation. Why wouldn't you practice this posture?

HOW TO DO IT:

Before I describe the posture, remember that your spine is divided into three parts. The Lumbar, or lower back, the Thoracic, or mid back, and the Cervical, the neck section. Generally, when you perform a twist, you will start at the base of your spine and slowly work your way up. I prefer to release the twist in the opposite order, top down (neck, mid-back, then low back), but you will find instructors that teach releasing the twist all at once, or from the bottom up. You might want to experiment and see which way you prefer. I think that as long as you get at least one good twist in a day, you can't go wrong with either method.

Start in Seated Mountain. The top of your head should be moving so much toward the ceiling that you feel as if your spine just grew another three inches. Place your right hand on the outside of your left thigh, and reach your left hand back behind you, either grabbing the side or back of the chair. Take a deep breath in, then as you exhale slowly turn your belly to the left. On your next exhale turn the chest farther to the left. With your next exhale you will deepen the twist as you involve your neck and upper back. Try to look back behind you. Take up to five breaths here, but with each inhale try to get the top of your head closer to the ceiling, and with each exhale try to deepen the twist. You can use your right hand to gently pull against your left thigh. This will help you deepen the twist.

When you are ready to release the twist, look forward as you inhale, then on a single exhale release first the chest forward, then the belly.

If you sit still for a moment, you will feel really lopsided. Sometimes the body asks for a Seated Cat or Cow before you go to the other side. Just listen and do what your body asks for. Then repeat the process, this time twisting to the right.

HOW TO SNEAK IT IN:

Twists can be very invigorating, so try to fit one of these in anytime you feel tired. I find this to be helpful in the middle of the afternoon, but you can do it anytime you feel sluggish. You can even do this in the carpool line as you're waiting for your kids to get out of school. Or how about when you get stuck in a traffic jam? If you can't change it, don't expend energy fighting it. Choose instead to do something beneficial for yourself with the unexpected "empty zone." Learn to use unexpected free time to your advantage.

Seated Hip Stretch

WHY SHOULD YOU PRACTICE THE SEATED HIP STRETCH?

Because this posture will increase the mobility of your hips and make them feel great! It stretches the gluteals and the piriformis muscle, a difficult muscle to access, and one that directly contributes to sciatic pain.

If you are or have ever been a runner, a cyclist, or a step-aerobic enthusiast, YOU NEED THIS STRETCH! If you sit at a desk all day long, YOU NEED THIS STRETCH!

HOW TO DO IT:

Begin in the Seated Mountain. Place your outer right ankle on your left thigh near the knee. Flex the right foot (drawing the toes back toward the knee) and gently move your right knee down toward the floor to stabilize it.

Take a deep breath in, then on your exhale hinge forward from the hips while keeping the front of the spine as long as you can. You will begin to feel a tugging sensation on your outer right hip area. Don't be alarmed if you don't seem to go down very far. Most people have really tight hips, so just do the best you can and **BREATHE.** You can place your hands on your hips, or you can reach them forward toward your desk, coffee table, or even down toward the floor. Take three to five breaths, or more if it feels really good.

This is an intense stretch for most people, so check to make sure that you aren't clenching your teeth.

When you are ready to come up, do so slowly on an inhale. Release the right leg and repeat on the other side. Remember that your sides can and will be different. Don't let that concern you. Just do the best you can on each side.

HOW TO SNEAK IT IN:

If you work in an office, it is worth setting an alarm for this exercise. Trust me, you will be glad you did. Or you can practice it with any regular "trigger" you have at work or home.

The Seated Hip Stretch is a great stretch to "sneak" in during TV commercials or time-outs during football or basketball games. I love this stretch and incorporate it as many times a day as I can!

Seated Deep Forward Fold

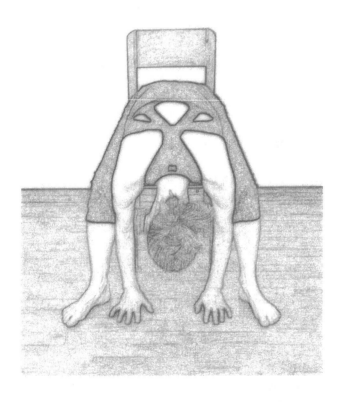

WHY SHOULD YOU PRACTICE THE SEATED DEEP FORWARD BEND?

Because this is a good one for your lower back, hips, and inner thighs. It can also help you release your jaw and neck. Plus, it has the added benefit of being a safe option in place of an inversion, which can be a boost to the circulatory and lymphatic systems.

If you have high blood pressure or glaucoma, however, you

will want to consult with your doctor to make sure this posture is safe for you.

HOW TO DO IT:

You need to begin sitting a little further back in your chair for this one because all of your weight will be sinking forward, and I don't want you to tip over! From the Seated Mountain posture, move your feet farther apart from each other, at least shoulder distance apart, maybe a little more. Make sure you have enough space between your legs for your belly to be able to sink down between your thighs. You can also turn your toes out a bit if that feels more comfortable to you.

Take a deep breath in and on your exhale hinge forward keeping your spine nice and straight. When you can't go down any farther with a straight spine slowly start rounding the back while sinking the belly down between the thighs, eventually releasing the top of your head toward the floor. Let your arms dangle, and relax your shoulders. As you continue breathing, focus on relaxing your lower back as you exhale. Allow gravity to assist you by surrendering the weight of your head and shoulders. Stay for a least five breaths, more if it feels really good to your back and hips.

When you are ready to come out of the Seated Deep Forward Bend, **slowly** lift your head, then your chest, then gradually come up all the way. Do not be in a hurry to come out of this posture! Some people might experience a little dizziness after this exercise, so make sure you have several moments to be still before you have to stand up.

HOW TO SNEAK IT IN:

This is one I like doing during TV commercials while I'm vegging on the sofa. But you could always "accidentally" drop something at work and just happen to "sneak" it in as you are "looking" for it under your desk. Just don't hit your head on your desk as you come up!

CHAPTER FOUR
Floor Postures

Introduction to the Floor Postures

This chapter won't be for everyone. If you have difficulty getting down to the floor (and back up again) then just focus on the breathing, standing, and seated exercises. But if you have small children and you often find yourself down on the floor with them, or if you have the ability to get down there, then this chapter is for you!

Balasana, or Child (Relaxed)

WHY SHOULD YOU PRACTICE THE RELAXED CHILD?

Because this is one of the best stretches you can do for your back. It will also help you stretch the tops of your feet and ankles, as well as improve flexibility around the knees.

HOW TO DO IT:

Start on the floor on your hands and knees. Bring your big toes together but allow some space between your knees. Let your hips sink down closer to your heels. You would like for the tops of your feet to be flat on the floor, but this in not everyone's reality. If you can't get the tops of your feet flat, roll up a towel and place it on the floor under the tops of your ankles. That should relieve some of the pressure across the feet and make it more comfortable for you.

Once your hips are settled down, lower your forehead to the floor. Now if your forehead doesn't go down that far, don't worry. If it is close, just cross your arms under your forehead to provide a little support, and if that's not enough, roll up a large towel or blanket to place under your forehead. It is important that you can be relaxed in this exercise.

If you do not have your arms under your forehead, you can extend them forward or you can place your hands by your feet with your palms turned up.

The trick to this posture is to breathe into your back. From the breathing chapter, you know that your breath can move around. This means that you can consciously direct it to various parts of your body. So in this position you want to direct your breath to your mid and low back area. Imagine that your lungs are where your kidneys are. Breathe deeply, and as you exhale let the crease at the hips get softer. Allow your hips to feel very heavy. Also, try to relax your shoulders and your knees.

When you are ready to come up, simply reach your hands forward and press them into the floor as you lift yourself back up to all fours.

HOW TO SNEAK IT IN:

Like I said earlier, these floor postures won't be for everyone. But if you find yourself on the floor with your children, then this one is easy to "sneak" in. Because the shape of the body resembles a turtle in the Relaxed Child, you can even have them join in the fun!

There was a time in my life when I had some chronic back issues. I kept a blanket under my bed and first thing every morning

I would go down to the floor in this posture. It was a life saver. And five to ten deep breaths in this posture is a gentle way to transition from the sleep world to the real one.

Balasana, or Child (Active)

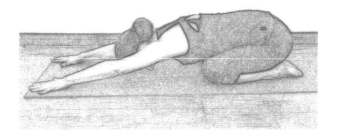

WHY SHOULD YOU PRACTICE THE ACTIVE CHILD?

Because this posture will address tightness in the upper back and shoulder area while still taking care of your lower back. And because it is so similar to the relaxed version, it can be a natural extension of the previous posture.

HOW TO DO IT:

Begin in the Relaxed Child position. Really feel the weight of your hips sink down, then start walking your hands forward away from the hips. Do not take your hips with you! The hips are sinking in one direction and the hands are moving in the opposite direction.

Once you get your hands as far away from you as you can, your arms should be straight and your elbows should be off the floor. Spread your fingers really wide apart and press all four corners of your palms into the floor, especially that stubborn mound at the base of your index fingers. You should now feel increased activity in your upper back and where your arms attach to your torso. You will have a nice, long waist.

Because your mid back will be in a stretched out position you will want to direct your breath to your side ribs. You can easily sneak in a side stretch if you walk your hands as far to the right as you can for a couple of breaths, then walk them over to the left for a couple of breaths. Just remember to keep the hands actively pressing down to get the most out of this position.

To exit the posture make sure your arms are reaching forward as you lift yourself up to an all-fours, or tabletop, position.

HOW TO SNEAK IT IN:

Again, this is a great one to sneak in if you have kids because you can encourage them to "play" along with you. Children love it when we adults get down on their level, so if you have the opportunity, have some fun in the Child posture and its variations with a real child. You get to spend some quality time with them and you get to do something positive for your body at the same time. Everybody wins!

Setu Bandha Sarvangasana, or Bridge

WHY SHOULD YOU PRACTICE THE BRIDGE?

Because this is a great way to work on both sides of the body at the same time. On the backside, you will strengthen your back, your glutes, and your hamstrings, while on the front side you will stretch the chest and shoulders, as well as the hip flexors and the quads.

This posture will also calm the nervous system and help tame an overactive brain. Although the posture requires a lot of effort when you are in it, most people feel very relaxed and experience a lower level of stress after they practice it.

HOW TO DO IT:

Begin on your back. Place your feet flat on the floor close to your hips, about hip distance apart. You want your feet to be parallel, just as if you were standing in the Mountain position.

When you are ready, press your feet into the floor and raise your hips off the floor toward the ceiling. If you can get your hips in line with your shoulders and your knees, then great! If not, great! Just go as far as you can. Keep your thighs parallel to each other, like railroad tracks. You do not want your knees moving out to the sides or knocking together. Keep your feet totally flat without rolling onto the outer edges of the feet.

One way to accentuate the stretch across the thighs is to consciously try to move your knees a little farther away from your hips. Of course, you won't get very far, but you should feel a nice stretch on the tops of the legs and also around the knees as you try.

One word of caution. You should NEVER turn your head to the side while in this posture. NEVER! And if you do feel any strain in the neck, try pressing the back of your head into the floor. If that doesn't alleviate your discomfort then come down. You can try again not raising the hips so high.

When you are ready to come out, simply lower the hips back down to the floor. You should then go into a Relaxed Little Boat, which is the next posture in the book.

HOW TO SNEAK IT IN:

This is a good one if you do aerobics, run, cycle, or sit for long periods, so try to "sneak" it in after a step or abdominals class (you're already there, so why not?) or after a long run or bike ride. You could even have your child push her toy cars under your "bridge" as you practice.

Aim for five to ten breaths in this position. It's amazing how this relatively simple backbend can make the front of the hips feel so good. You may even notice an increase in your stride after consistently sneaking this one in.

Pavanamuktasana, or Little Boat (Relaxed)

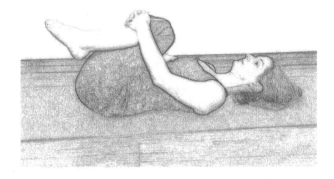

WHY SHOULD YOU PRACTICE THE RELAXED LITTLE BOAT?

Because, along with the Child posture, this is a great exercise if you tend to have lower back issues. It is basically the Child position upside down, so if you have knee problems that prevent you from practicing the Child, then this is a great alternative for you. It is also a counter posture for the Bridge because it restores length to the lower back.

This posture is sometimes referred to as the "Wind Relieving Pose," so it can be of help if you are having digestive issues.

HOW TO DO IT:

Lie on your back and pull your knees up to your chest. That's about it! Take several deep breaths and consciously relax your lower back and hips as you exhale. You can even gently rock side to side if it feels good to you.

HOW TO SNEAK IT IN:

As I stated in the Bridge section, this is a counter posture to that backbend, so sneak this one in after you practice the Bridge. And if you are on the floor with your young child, maybe he could fill your "boat" with his favorite toys.

Pavanamuktasana, or Little Boat (Active)

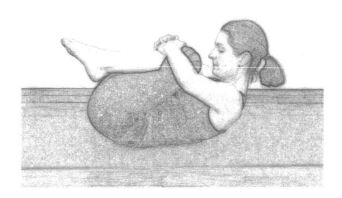

WHY SHOULD YOU PRACTICE THE ACTIVE LITTLE BOAT?

Because this more active version of Little Boat will give your abdominals, your arms, and your shoulders a nice little workout without straining the back.

HOW TO DO IT:

Start in the relaxed version of Little Boat. Interlace your fingers and place your hands at the top of your shins right below the knees. Take a deep breath in and as you exhale use your arm strength to pull your knees as close to your chest as possible. Flexing your feet will give the Achilles a nice stretch.

Now is when the real work starts. Keep your arms active by continuing to pull against the knee area. Lift your elbows and move them away from each other, toward opposite walls. Once you do this action you should feel your chest and upper back get involved.

If you do not have neck problems, you can then tuck your chin toward your chest and move your forehead toward your knees. You should be in a tight, tucked ball position with your elbows extending away from each other. Engage the abdominals, pressing them down toward the floor.

Because your abdominal region is engaged in this position, you will need to consciously direct your breath to your side ribs while in the Active Little Boat.

After several breaths, lower the head back down to the floor and slowly release the tension in the arms. Then return the feet back to the floor.

HOW TO SNEAK IT IN:

If you are able to get down on the floor first thing in the morning, this is a really nice way to wake up the body and start generating some heat. If you are down on the floor with your children ask them what this posture reminds them of. Maybe a bug on its back? A sleeping upside down turtle? An empty peanut shell? Encourage them to use their imagination and then have them imitate you.

Little Boat Twist

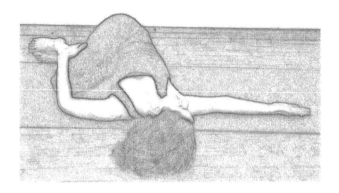

WHY SHOULD YOU PRACTICE THE LITTLE BOAT TWIST?

Because this posture will help you increase the flexibility of your mid and lower back while opening the shoulders and chest. And because it's a twist, it can help stimulate the internal organs, aiding in digestion.

HOW TO DO IT:

Start in the Relaxed Little Boat. With the knees up near the chest, place your right hand on the outside of the left knee. Take a deep inhale, then on the exhale let your right hand guide your knees all the way down to the floor to your right. You would like for your knees to stay tucked close to your body if possible. Imagine that your knees are trying to get closer to your armpit area. This helps elongate the lower back.

Extend your left arm out to the side, and if it feels all right to your neck, you can gently turn your head to the left, looking toward your left hand. Release the left shoulder as close to the floor as possible.

Breathe deeply into the left side of your ribcage, waist and hip. When you are ready to come out, recenter your head, then bring your knees back up to the original Little Boat position. Realign your spine, then repeat on the other side.

HOW TO SNEAK IT IN:

This twist is a natural extension of the previous two postures, so tack it on at the end of those if you can. We need more twists in our lives, and this is a doable one, especially if you are already down on the floor. Besides, it will only add another 45 seconds, so why not?

Conclusion

I hope that this book will encourage you to "sneak" a little more yoga into your daily life. It's not difficult to do if you remember to utilize your "empty zones" and pay attention to your "triggers." If you are currently taking classes, I encourage you to continue. The exercises and suggestions in this book are not meant to be a replacement for a class, but a complement to one.

If you are not currently enrolled in a yoga class, I strongly urge you to consider taking one. You cannot see yourself properly while in a posture to adequately gauge your form, and form is an extremely important aspect of the practice, especially when it comes to preventing injuries down the road. Yoga is a skill-based practice, so you want to hone your skills under the watchful eyes of a qualified teacher if at all possible.

Most of all, have fun with your yoga! Yoga is an uplifting and inspiring endeavor, and who doesn't need more inspiration in the midst of daily life?

If you enjoyed *How to Sneak More Yoga Into Your Life*, please check out its companion book, *How to Sneak More Meditation Into Your Life: A Doable Meditation Plan for Busy People*.

Thank you for reading my book!

Namaste.

About the Author

K. Kris Loomis has been teaching and learning from her yoga students for almost 20 years. She has studied yoga with David Swenson, Esther Myers, Stephanie Keach, and Sean Corn. Kris is the author of another nonfiction book, *How to Sneak More Meditation Into Your Life: A Doable Meditation Plan for Busy People*, as well as the the fiction series, "Modern Shorts for Busy People." Kris is a classically trained pianist, a determined chess player, an origami enthusiast, and a playwright.

Visit Kris' website at www.kkrisloomis.com and receive a free short story! You can find her on Facebook, Twitter, and Pinterest.

One Last Thing

If you enjoyed *How to Sneak More Yoga Into Your Life* and found it useful, I'd be grateful if you'd post a short review on Amazon. Your support and comments really make a difference, especially to indie authors!

I would also appreciate good old fashioned "word of mouth" to your friends, colleagues, or anyone you think would benefit from having a little more yoga in their life.

Thanks again for your support!

Made in the USA
Columbia, SC
12 December 2017